FUEL

YOUR

Motivation

FUEL YOUR

Motivation

31 Daily Motivations to Keep You Moving Forward

Copyright © 2018 Shyron Brailey

Fuel Your Motivation :*31 Daily Motivations to Keep You Moving Forward*

Published by ZION Publishing House

Los Angeles & Washington, D. C.

www.zionpublishinghouse.com

ISBN: 978-0-9983845-6-6

All rights reserved. The author guarantees all contents are original and do not infringe upon the legal rights of any other person or work. No part of this book may be reproduced, distributed, or transmitted in any form or by any means – electronic, mechanical, digital, photocopy, recording, or any other—except for brief quotations in printed reviews, without the prior written permission of the publisher.

 Scriptures marked KJV are taken from the KING JAMES VERSION (KJV): KING JAMES VERSION, public domain.

 Scriptures marked NIV are taken from the NEW INTERNATIONAL VERSION (NIV): Scripture taken from THE HOLY BIBLE, NEW INTERNATIONAL VERSION ®. Copyright© 1973, 1978, 1984, 2011 by Biblica, Inc.™. Used by permission of Zondervan

Printed in the United States of America

CONTENTS

INTRODUCTION 11

DAY 1 15

~Live on Purpose~

DAY 2 19

~Live on Purpose~

DAY 3 23

~Live on Purpose~

DAY 4 25

~What Are You Passionate About?~

DAY 5 29

~"Pregnant" With Purpose~

DAY 6 33

~What Are You Waiting For?~

DAY 7 35

~Pain and Pursuing Your Purpose~

DAY 8 37

~Dealing With Discouragement~

DAY 9 39

~Defusing Distractions~

DAY 10: 43

~Time Robbers~

DAY 11 47

~Surviving Your Preparation Season~

DAY 12 51

~Surviving Your Preparation Season~

DAY 13 55

~Surviving Your Preparation Season~

DAY 14 59

~Surviving Your Preparation Season~

DAY 15 61

~Detox~

DAY 16 65

~Warning Signs~

DAY 17 69

~Be Intentional~

DAY 18.. 71

~Declutter~

DAY 19.. 73

~In Pursuit of Your Purpose~

DAY 20.. 77

~The Importance of Balance~

DAY 21.. 81

~The Power of Choice~

DAY 22.. 85

~It's Time to Evict Fear and Doubt~

DAY 23.. 89

~Be YOU~

DAY 24.. 93

~Fuel Your Motivation~

DAY 25.. 97

~Be Unstoppable!!~

DAY 26.. 101

~Confidence Builder~

DAY 27 105

~Temperature Check~

DAY 28 109

~Don't Give Up~

DAY 29 113

~Last Lap~

DAY 30 115

~It's Time for Some Action!~

DAY 31 117

~A Driving Force Behind Success~

"ARE YOU COMMITTED?" 121

THE POWER OF ENCOURAGEMENT 125

A SPECIAL THANKS 127

ABOUT THE AUTHOR 129

Fuel Your Motivation

31 Daily Motivations to Keep You Moving Forward

Coaching For Success is all about raising awareness regarding your purpose, and then equipping & empowering you to Move Forward to success, while helping you live a balanced life in both the natural and spiritual realms.

Move Forward

I want to encourage you to continue "moving forward." Continue to pursue your dreams. Focus your time and energy on things that line up with your vision and purpose. The only person with the power to stop you…is you! So, get a tenacious and relentless mindset and move toward your dreams.

I am excited about your future!

INTRODUCTION

Be Resolved

This year, don't make resolutions but be resolved!

Resolutions are things that you are <u>considering</u> doing this year.

Being resolved is an already made-up mind, knowing what will be done this year.
Resolved - *to make a firm decision about; to remove or dispel doubts.*

<u>A, Resolution Mindset</u>
1. Considers or vacillates
2. Has no accountability
3. Makes excuses
4. Procrastinates

<u>B. Resolved Mindset</u>
1. Determined to achieve
2. Has accountability
3. Has a "no exception" policy
4. Is about "action!"

1. How do I know which mindset I have?

By your attitude, actions, and your speech

If I have a **Resolution Mindset**, I will:

- Want a closer relationship with God
- Want to get out of debt
- Want to lose weight

If I have a **Resolved Mindset**, I will:

- Develop a closer walk with God. I will make spending time with God a priority.
- Be Debt Free by having a plan to pay off debts and start saving.
- Lose weight. I will join a gym, get a trainer, buy a treadmill, get a walking buddy, and change my eating habits.

2. How do I shift from a Resolution Mindset to a Resolved Mindset?

- **Have an action plan**
- *"Write the vision and make it plain......."* Habakkuk 2:2 (KJV). Create a vision board. Ask yourself, "What am I trying to accomplish?" "In what time frame do I want to accomplish this?"
- **Be accountable**
- Have someone who you can give a "progress report" or an update of your advancement.

This should be a person who will help keep you on track, encouraged, and motivated.
- **Don't make excuses--make adjustments**
- This is how you hurdle obstacles. This is also how you keep your motivation fueled.

This year be resolved. **Make this a year of action!** Expect the great!

Reflection Page: *Write down what you will be resolved about this year.*

DAY 1

~LIVE ON PURPOSE~

We have all asked questions, such as, "What is my purpose?" "Why was I created?" Some of you may have even read the powerful book, *Purpose Driven Life* by Rick Warren. But, what does it mean to live on purpose?

Here are Five Points to "Live on Purpose."

1. Living on purpose means you surrender all your will to God.

Your will is to do the will of the Father. You have taken on the attitude of Christ who says, *"Yet not as I will, but as you will"* Matthew 26:39b (New International Version). This mindset makes it easy to hear and obey what the Holy Spirit tells you to do, knowing that God is with you every step of the way. You can walk with a holy confidence because you know it was God that *"willed this in you to do,"* according to Philippians 2:13. God has promised to complete the good work He placed in you. *"Being confident of this, that he who began a good work in you will carry it on to completion until the day of Christ Jesus"* Philippians 1:6 (NIV).

2. Living on purpose is knowing God has a plan for your life.

You are <u>not</u> an accident! Your birth did not catch God off guard. God created you with a specific purpose in mind. *"For I know the plans I have for you, declares the Lord, plans to prosper you and not to harm you, plans to give you hope and a future"* Jeremiah 29:11 (NIV). God knew you before you were formed in your mother's womb and had already mapped out your life and purpose. Look at Jeremiah 1:5. You need to <u>know and believe</u> this to "live on purpose."

If you don't know, seek and ask God **what He has placed in you to share with the world for His glory.** Then, live each day under *"the guidance of the Holy Spirit who will guide you into all truth"*, according to John 16:13. God sent the Holy Spirit to dwell in us and lead us according to His will and plan for our life.

Reflection Page: *Write down what you discovered by surrendering to God. Do you believe God has a plan for your life? What is your purpose?*

DAY 2

~LIVE ON PURPOSE~

3. Living on purpose means you don't live your life <u>comparing</u> yourself to others.

Living on purpose means you know who you are based on what God has said about you in His Word. Yes, *"you are fearfully and wonderfully made!"* (See Psalms 139:14). You know the assignment God has for you, only you can do. God purposefully and strategically created your personality and abilities to fulfill your assignment. You know how to stay in your "lane" and follow the leading of the Holy Spirit. God has your time and season already prepared. (See 1 Corinthians 2:9). All you must do is obey!

Don't look at other people and see how far along they are ahead of you (especially those doing the same thing you are doing). In your eyes, it may seem or look as if you aren't making progress. Remember, God has a "set time and a set people" for you! There is a remnant of people just for you. People that only you will be able to reach. Comparing yourself to others causes you to lose focus, lose ground, and <u>causes delays</u>. Instead, celebrate with those who are fulfilling their purpose and the will of God. Your time is coming! You will want others to celebrate with you when your time comes.

I often use the example of a "place setting" at a dinner table. You have a plate, bowl, glass, silverware, and napkin. In their proper (or purposed) place, they are beautiful and effective. But, when they try to be something they were not created to be, they make a mess. It is the same with us. When we compare ourselves to others and try to be anything or anyone other than what God created us to uniquely be, WE MAKE A MESS!

Reflection Page: *Do you find you are comparing yourself to others? Do you now understand the danger of comparison? How will you "stay in your lane?"*

DAY 3

~LIVE ON PURPOSE~

4. **Living on purpose means you don't allow fear to stop you.**

You don't allow <u>fear or negative people</u> stop you from doing what God has told you or tells you to do. Fear causes doubt and will make you begin to question what God has already told you. **Don't allow fear and doubt to paralyze you!** Don't allow it to keep you from moving forward. Put *fear* in its place. (See 2 Timothy 1:7). Be about your Father's business! *"We must obey God rather than human beings!"* Acts 5:29 (NIV).

5. **Living on purpose means you live a fulfilled life!**

When you walk in the will of God, you experience true happiness and fulfillment. You will not live a fulfilled life until you are doing the will of God. (See John 15:10-11). The questions to ask yourself are, "What is God's will for my life?" & "What does God want me doing in this season of my life?" This way you are not just "acting" busy, but you are effective and enjoying every day life as you "Live on Purpose."

Reflection Page: *What should you be doing in this season of your life?*

DAY 4

~WHAT ARE YOU PASSIONATE ABOUT?~

What is it you love to do? What is it that causes you to be excited inside? Whatever you are passionate about is not considered work for you. You do it effortlessly, and you enjoy doing it. What seems hard for others, you're able to complete with ease. You would even do the activity without pay. Speaking about your passion is something you can do at any given moment without prior notice or script.

Many times, your passion comes from the experiences you have gone through. What are some things that bother you? Whatever bothers you may be the thing you are called to as part of your purpose. For example, you may love to organize events, and when you see things out of order, it drives you crazy! Immediately, you begin to think how the event could have been done and run more smoothly. This suggests you may be passionate about order and organization and most likely have the gift or talents for Event Planning or Administration.

Passionate: *Capable of or having intense feelings; showing or expressing strong emotion.*

Your passion is linked to your purpose. There are abilities (gifts or talents) that you are equipped with which will enable you to flourish when used within your niche. There is a great feeling of fulfillment when you *work your niche*! This is what you were predestined to do. **This is also where you will be most effective**. By being in your "lane," you will feel a sense of relevance and impact. Discover your passion and *"stir up the gift that is within you."* (See 2 Timothy 1:6).

Reflection Page: *What things are you passionate about? What gifts have been stirred up in you?*

DAY 5

~"PREGNANT" WITH PURPOSE~

Have you ever felt something deep inside of you, letting you know there is more that you have to do? It's as if something is trapped in a cage and needs to be set free. A lot of us are "pregnant with purpose." Purpose is kicking us, reminding us it is still there. You did not abort! Your purpose is growing and preparing for delivery. You just don't know the "due date."

Some of us are just like Sarah, full of doubt. When the angel of the Lord prophesied to her about having a son, she laughed. Look at Genesis 18:10-15. Why? Because Sarah was looking at the natural and not the supernatural in her current circumstances. Her circumstances, in no way, "lined up" with what the angel was saying. Sarah was old and well past child-bearing age. Abraham was old and not able to produce. But, when God says IT, IT shall come to pass!

You are pregnant (filled) with purpose. Some of you are way past your due date. You have been delaying, putting off your purpose. Some of you thought you aborted or miscarried, but the baby is moving and kicking!

It's time to PUSH!

What has God told you or showed you in a dream, and you are laughing because of your circumstances? Is there anything too hard for the Lord? The answer is, "NO!" So, STOP laughing and have the baby!

Reflection Page: *What is it you need to deliver? Will you stop laughing (looking at your circumstances and making excuses) and just have the baby?*

DAY 6

~WHAT ARE YOU WAITING FOR?~

It's time to get going! It's time to get rid of fear and procrastination! It's time to stop making excuses!

Don't rely on what you see and how you feel. Your "vision" and "feelings" are not reliable. Your eyes will trick you, and your feelings are flaky. They go up and down. Rely only on the Word of God! What has God said about you and your situation? *Walk by faith and not by sight* and most definitely not by emotions! Trust God. He cannot lie, and His promises are, "Yes" and "Amen!" God wants the BEST for you!

It's time to get that thing done that you have been putting off! You know you have to do it, but for some reason, you just can't seem to get going. Don't let another year go by with you haven't started. What is hindering you from moving forward? Is it fear? Fear of failure or success? Are you feeling inadequate? Are you comparing yourself with others? Are you procrastinating? Whatever it is, I pray that <u>today you will have the desire, zeal, and motivation to step out and get started.</u> Do it afraid! Speak life to your dreams and listen to the people who will fuel your passion for your purpose!

I challenge you to get started this week. The furthest point from the finish line is the starting line.

Reflection Page: *What will you start this week?*

DAY 7

~PAIN AND PURSUING YOUR PURPOSE~

Opposition and distractions will come as you pursue your purpose (the thing or things that God told you to do). But, can you pursue through your pain? Will you allow your circumstances to stop you? You have to press, push, and continue to pursue after your dreams in order to get where God is taking you. **Quitting is not an option!** Reaping comes if you do not faint.

I always say, "Nothing is wasted with God." So, no matter where you are today, know that where you are and what you have been through has been strategically woven into your life's purpose. Ask yourself, "What is the lesson I need to learn from this situation?" "How will I grow from this experience?" Keep moving forward! There is a blessing in your pressing.

Pain Pushes You – Pain Positions You – & Pain can be turned into PRAISE. Pain precedes and promotes PROGRESS. Every successful person can tell you a story behind their progress. We see the glory, but we don't know the story. **Don't allow your pain to stop you from pursuing your purpose!**

Reflection Page: *What opposition or challenges are you facing? What is the "gift" from your pain?*

DAY 8

~DEALING WITH DISCOURAGEMENT~

When you get discouraged with whatever you are doing, think about WHY you are doing it. WHY did you want to start the business? WHY did you want to write the book? WHY did you want to go back to school?

Remembering WHY you started in the first place should refuel your motivation to continue your pursuit. I became a "Life Coach" because I love helping people! I love to see people grow and live a balanced & fulfilled life. I love seeing people doing what they were created and gifted to do. I love seeing others living life on purpose!

I encourage you to celebrate your different stages of success! This will help and act as "fuel for motivation" to keep you moving forward. Sometimes we are too hard on ourselves, and we never acknowledge the things we have done or achieved. You need to plan how you will celebrate each stage of your success. If you need someone to hold you accountable to do this, I will. I or others can celebrate with you.

Don't be discouraged. Be Inspired. May you have a renewed passion for your vision today!

Reflection Page: *Write down why you started doing what you're doing. Plan your celebratory stages. Who will help you be accountable?*

DAY 9

~DEFUSING DISTRACTIONS~

Have you noticed every time you set your mind to do anything, something pops up? I mean, out of nowhere, and most times it doesn't even make sense. These situations or occurrences are called **distractions**. Any time you truly set your mind to do anything (especially something attached to your purpose), you can be sure distractions will come.

How do you defuse distractions?

You have to have a made-up mind about what you want to accomplish.

You can't be vacillating back and forth about what you want. You have to be resolved! You must be determined. You have to say, "I am going to complete _____ (fill in the blank) no matter what comes up or is thrown at me." That way, when those *out of the blue* situations arise, you are already aware about them and prepared. You knew they were coming, and you've already **resolved you would not be distracted!** You continue to move forward and complete your assignment.

You have to know how you are going to react to distractions.

You're not going to be surprised or taken advantage of. (See 2 Corinthians 2:11). Once you've made up your mind to do a thing and realize distractions are coming, you should be on guard and ready to respond **not out of emotion but out of wisdom.**

You have to <u>not</u> stop the work!

The prophet, Nehemiah in the Bible, showed us a good example of how not to allow distractions to cause us to stop our work. Look at Nehemiah Chapter 6. You need to tell your distractions, i.e., people and/or situations, you will not "come down" or stop the work. Nehemiah even asked those trying to distract him this question in Nehemiah 6:3, *"Why should the work stop while I leave it and go down to you?* (NIV). We know Nehemiah wasn't coming down, but he wanted those trying to distract him to know that he knew their motives. This **<u>defused</u>** their attempts! They were only distractions to keep him from completing his work.

You have to not entertain foolishness!

Foolishness is a "time robber" and an "energy drainer!" Don't waste your time or energy entertaining foolishness. It is designed to distract you and cause you to stop working on your work. And, if not to stop the work completely, at least to delay it. Ignore foolishness and put the time and energy into completing your assignment and achieving your goals. Proverbs 26:4, *"Do not answer a fool according to his folly, or you yourself will be just like him."* (NIV).

BECOME SKILLED AT DEFUSING DISTRACTIONS!

Reflection Page: *Identify your distractions. How will you "defuse" them?*

DAY 10:

~TIME ROBBERS~

We often say, "I don't have enough time, or I don't have any time to do that." Do you really not have time, or are you not managing your time effectively? Do an evaluation of your days and nights for about a week and see what you are doing with your time. I did this recently and discovered two important things about time:

1. *People don't value your time*

2. *People don't manage their time*

There is a saying that *time is money*. Don't let people waste your time! Make them respect your time.

You be on time. Make the most of the time that you have. If a person doesn't respect your time, then there shouldn't be a next time. This is time you could have been productively working on your own dreams and goals, instead of allowing someone else to waste your time.

One other thing I discovered is we spend lots of time doing non-productive things. Not that there is anything wrong with this, but "it" needs to be managed. Some boundaries need to be set. Some examples of non-productive things:

- *Television*
- *Social Media, i.e. Facebook*
- *Cell phones*
- *Video games*

Instead of watching three hours of TV, you can use that time or divide that time working on your dreams or goals. This goes for any of the above. This is not a complete list, of course, just some examples. Too much time given to these *time robbers* "eats up" and lessens the time you can give to your dreams. They also delay you from getting things done and seeing your vision come to fruition.

Reflection Page: *Identify your "time robbers." How much time are you spending on them? Write down the boundaries you will set. Do you need accountability in this area?*

DAY 11

~SURVIVING YOUR PREPARATION SEASON~

During your "Season of Preparation," don't <u>despise where you are</u>! Where you are is the place designed to equip you with some skills and knowledge for where God is taking you. You will miss out on your preparation season if all you do is complain. Get the lessons, skills, and knowledge you need to complete your journey and thank God for taking the time to thoroughly equip you before sending you out. Let's look at four tips to help you survive during your season of preparation.

Four C's to Surviving Your Season of Preparation

1. Commune with God

Consistent fellowship with God is <u>vital</u> during your season of preparation! This is not the time to "slack off" or stop going to church or Bible study. This is a time you should cling to God and the things of God. Prayer time, reading God's Word, meditation, and journal writing should be a daily priority.

This is a time of one-on-one tutoring from the Holy Spirit. This is a time of heightened discernment and a keen ear to hear God's voice and receive clear instructions. This is a very special time as you get thoroughly equipped for where God is preparing you to go and what He has in store for you.

Reflection Page: *As you spend time communing with God, write down what you hear Him saying.*

DAY 12

~SURVIVING YOUR PREPARATION SEASON~

2. Control your emotions

One of the most effective ways to control your emotions is to cast down negative thoughts and replace them with the Word of God. (See 2 Cor. 10:5). We have already been advised to renew our minds daily according to Romans 12:2 *"Do not conform to the pattern of this world but be transformed by the renewing of your mind...."* (NIV). This will be critical during your season of preparation. Casting down negativity and dwelling instead on God's Word will be vital, for <u>you will be dealing with emotions of loneliness, being overlooked, rejection, abandonment, being forgotten, feelings of irrelevance, and being unqualified,</u> just to name a few.

When we look at different people from the Bible, they all went through a season or seasons of preparation, and I'm sure they battled these same emotions. Moses went from the Egyptian palace to the wilderness. I'm sure he was very lonely on the backside of Midian and felt forgotten. But, this was his season of preparation. Moses needed this time to learn who God was and to get clear instructions on what God wanted him to do. Look at Exodus 3:1-10.

Moses, feeling unqualified, made excuses just like we do. **Moses communed with God and received one-on-one teaching and instructions from Yahweh during this period**. Moses was being equipped to be a shepherd of God's people.

I'm sure David felt overlooked. (See 1 Samuel 16:6-12). In this biblical account, David's father didn't even consider him when Samuel asked to see all his sons, regarding becoming the future king of Israel.

Joseph had to deal with close family hurt during his preparation season. He faced abandonment and rejection, as his brothers threw him in a ditch and then sold him.

Moses, David, and Joseph were called to greatness! <u>**Every part of their lives prepared and equipped them for that greatness**</u>. Don't despise where you are or what you are going through. God has strategically weaved events into your life with a divine purpose. God has to get some things out of us and put some things in us. **Nothing is wasted with God!** Every aspect of your life has been <u>intentionally orchestrated to prepare and equip you for your divine purpose</u>.

Reflection Page: *What are some emotions you are dealing with? How will you manage them? (Find scriptures to dispel the "lie" of your emotions)*

DAY 13

~SURVIVING YOUR PREPARATION SEASON~

3. Choose your "inner circle" wisely

You don't need negative people or "dream drainers" in your ear.
<u>Under this survival technique, you will have to "cut off" or limit the amount of time you spend with people who are not profitable for you during your season of preparation.</u> During this season, since it is already easy for you to want to quit and "throw in the towel," you don't need others helping you to make that decision easy by their negative comments. Remember, *misery loves company*. If they aren't doing anything or making any significant moves in their life, they most likely don't want you to, either. These people have two things going on with them which are affecting their life and their attitude.

1. *They have no vision.*
2. *They struggle with jealousy and comparing themselves with others.*
    Pray for them and keep it moving. You still love them, but in this preparation season, you don't need and can't afford their negativity, added to what you are already dealing with.

There is a saying, "**Go where you will be celebrated and not tolerated.**"
You need to have positive people around you who know the Word and will remind you that the promises of God are, "Yes" and "Amen." This will encourage you *"not to be weary in well doing"* for you know, *"<u>in due season</u> you will reap, if you faint not."* From Galatians 6:9. You also need to have people around you, you trust and can be accountable to. Next to handling your emotions, having the right inner- circle can make or break you! Your "inner circle" can either positively support you or be your biggest distraction. Guard your ear gates and don't allow your ears to be polluted with lies. Combat lies with the TRUTH, which is the Word of God!

It is comforting to know even Joseph's brothers could not stop his dream that God had given him from coming true despite their efforts. **Neither can your God-given dreams be stopped by man!**

Reflection Page: *Who is in your inner-circle? Are they dream catchers or dream drainers? Write their names down. Write down if they push you toward your goals or delay you from reaching them.*

DAY 14

~SURVIVING YOUR PREPARATION SEASON~

4. Close your eyes to comparison

Your preparation season is <u>not</u> the same time frame as anybody else's. God knows what needs to come *out of us* and what we need to be *filled* with. He also knows how long this process will take. **God knows how to thoroughly equip us for where He is taking us**. We all have to travel our own road. We each have different ETA's (Estimated Times of Arrival). Don't waste time looking at where other people are or how far along they appear to be. If we say we believe Jeremiah 29:11, then we need to act like we believe.

Your actions will show if you truly believe this or not. You will start to jump ahead of God in anxiety or lag behind Him, in procrastination. This will cause you to get out of sync in your walk with God because you will have gotten out of your lane.

Trust God's plan and <u>timing</u>! He knows what is best for us, and when it is best for us to do what He has created and called us to do. You will have "contentment" and "peace" by not comparing yourself to others and by trusting God knows what He is doing.

Reflection Page: *Do you find that you are comparing yourself to others? Why is it important to stay in your lane? How will you check yourself when you realize you are comparing?*

DAY 15

~DETOX~

Are there some things or people in your life who are toxic to your growth and progress? Sometimes, we want something so badly, we fail to heed any hazard (or warning) signs. Most often, we don't pay any attention to them until it is too late, and the damage is already done. These hazardous things, people, or events impede your progress, and sometimes if not removed quickly, will kill your dreams.

Do a self-examination and see what hazardous (poisonous & toxic) issues you have in your life that are hindering you from moving forward. Here are some examples: negativity, negative people, negative talking, negative expectations, and fear. I call these "vision blockers."

<u>Remove all the hazardous things or people from your life,</u> so you can move forward!

Take a daily antibiotic, (the Word of God) and reject anything that is anti-Christ! If something doesn't line up with what God has said, it is no good for you and needs to be removed from your life and out of your system. **This is especially true for your system of thinking**.

Renew your mind daily! As I mentioned earlier, guard your "ear gates," and you must also watch the words that come out of your own mouth. Speak Life! *"For we walk by faith, not by sight!"* 2 Cor. 5:7 (King James Version). Allow the blood of Jesus to rid you of all toxic and hazardous issues in your life. There is wonder-working power in the blood of Jesus. By His stripes you are healed!

Reflection Page: *Identify the toxic people or things in your life. Then, detox.*

DAY 16

~WARNING SIGNS~

Are you ignoring the "warning" signs? When a light on your car dashboard comes on, whether it's for your fuel, engine, or door, do you ignore the warning sign, or do you take the appropriate action necessary and get whatever needs to be fixed, checked out? Sometimes, it's an easy fix, i.e., the trunk may not be closed all the way. Nevertheless, you have a choice to either ignore the "sign" or take heed and take action. Most of the situations we find ourselves in, if we are honest, happen because we ignore the warning signs to correct the problem. With every choice there are consequences. Just like in the car example, you can ignore the FUEL light and keep driving, but eventually, you are going to run out of gas someplace and be stuck or stranded.

The purpose of warning signs or a warning sign is to help us avoid something that may be dangerous for us or not profitable for where we are going. The Holy Spirit alerts us to people, places, and things that will take us out of alignment with God and His purpose for our life. When we don't take heed to the "warning," it causes delays in fulfilling our purpose.

Band Aid vs. Surgery Theory

Do you try to put a Band-Aid on situations which need surgery? Ignoring the situation won't make it go away. Patching it up is only a temporary solution; the problem is still there. It will be back. Facing your giant is the only way to receive true deliverance or resolution for a situation.

Don't ignore "warning" signs! Pay attention and save yourself time, money, hurt, and stress.

Reflection Page: *What "warning" signs are you ignoring?*

DAY 17

~BE INTENTIONAL~

Do something today that lines up with what you need to get done. Ask yourself, "Does this help me move forward in accomplishing my goals?" "Is what I'm doing profitable for me for what I'm trying to do, or is this just a distraction?" Don't waste time. Value your time and other people's time. **We spend a lot of time being busy but not effective**. This is because we are not "intentional" in our plans and actions.

Plan – what you are going to do, how you will spend your time, and who you need to meet with

Prepare – so you are ready when the opportunity comes

Pursue – it's not enough to think about doing something or even to just talk about doing something, you have to "be about" doing that thing. Go after your dreams!

Start today thinking about what you are doing and stop just doing things carelessly. Take yourself off "cruise control" and be the driver of your destiny.

Reflection Page: *What will you do this week that specifically aligns with your dreams?*

DAY 18

~DECLUTTER~

Declutter. *To remove mess or clutter from a place; to organize and prioritize (one's commitments, material possessions)*

There are times in life when we need to "declutter" our minds as well as our surroundings, i.e., home and work areas. The benefit of decluttering is it brings clarity! It's hard to see or think clearly when there is so much "stuff," i.e., too many thoughts obstructing your view. Your answer could be right in front of you, but you won't see it because of all the clutter.

After removing all the clutter, you are able to see what is left and can create order. You will be able to organize what is left which will help you work more efficiently and effectively. When there is order, you can perform in a spirit of excellence.

Reflection Page: *Do you need to declutter?*

DAY 19

~IN PURSUIT OF YOUR PURPOSE~

I want to make you aware of some things you will face while in "'pursuit of your purpose." When you are in *pursuit of something*, you are focused on that target. Your mind isn't on anything else. The enemy can't stop your purpose, so he attempts to stop you by any means necessary!

When you are in pursuit of purpose, opposition will come!

While you are pursuing your purpose, your enemies (or haters) will pursue you to try and stop you.

If you are waiting on your family members or those closest to you to support you in your pursuit of purpose, you will be disappointed. These are the ones who the enemy often uses to cause you to question what God has told you to do. Many times, this is where the enemy stops you.

God is not looking for excuses; He's looking for "increase" on what He placed inside of you.

When you are in pursuit of purpose, obedience is not an option!

You must learn to walk in extreme and immediate obedience to God. When God tells you to do something, just do it! When you don't act immediately, you allow your flesh to question what God is doing and bring about fear and doubt, instead of trusting God and doing what He said.

Don't allow your circumstances to paralyze you or stop you! Often when God tells us to do something or gives us a vision, we immediately begin to look at what's going on in the "natural." We start to say, "I don't have the money." "When will I have time?" "Who will help me?" **Your obedience is not based on your circumstances!** Most of the time when God asks you to do something, the conditions are **not** favorable. This ensures that He gets all the glory!

When you are in pursuit of purpose, there is no time for excuses!

There's no more time for just existing and not living on purpose. There's no more time for <u>not knowing your purpose!</u> Excuses stop you from having impact and relevance.

Seek God and ask Him, "What is my purpose?" "What was I created to do in the *hyphen* of my life, i.e., (birth-death)?" Could it be the very thing you've gone through is the thing you're called to? For example, I grew up in a blended family. I was a stepchild and understand how that feels. When I got married in 1991, we were a blended family. I didn't have any children yet, but I had two bonus children. When I remarried in 2008, my current husband, (Henry) and I, had both been divorced and had children from our previous marriages. There were eight of us when we got married. I called us, "God's Blended Best". Through experience as a child and a parent in a blended family, I am passionate about helping blended marriages and families. Your gift will make room for you and place you before great men. As long as you are pursuing your gift, there will be opportunities for you to affect other's lives. When your pursuit stops – the opportunities cease.

Once you know your purpose, you can begin to "walk on purpose," have more confidence, and be effective. You can live a fulfilled life! Fulfillment comes when you do what God created, pre-destined, and deliberately designed and equipped you to do.

So, when you find yourself making excuses, stop and make adjustments! You are well able to do whatever God has in store for you. Go and be great!

Reflection Page: *Start pursuing your purpose today!*

DAY 20

~THE IMPORTANCE OF BALANCE~

Being productive is great, but remember BALANCE is vital! Don't forget to put YOU on your calendar! Schedule some time with yourself. Relax, indulge in a hobby you enjoy, or spend time with a good friend or family member. Get away or go on a "stay-cation." Whatever allows you to rest and get restored is necessary to keeping your life in balance. Let's look at some ways to help you maintain your balance.

Three Keys to maintaining your balance

1. Don't overbook yourself

You are the keeper of your calendar. Take responsibility and manage your time. Balance keeps you stable and less stressed. We must balance a number of things; for instance, family, work or business, school, ministry, finances, and our health. Remember, every decision you make will affect your balance, either positively or negatively.

2. Delegate

I know you feel you have to do everything; but you don't. Allow others to help you. They may not do it exactly the way you would, but that's okay as long as they get the job done correctly.

Also, it is okay to say, "No." Most times, I think people feel badly when they have to tell someone *no*. But, if you *legitimately* are not able to do something, it is okay. Don't add additional stress to your life taking on things you won't be able to manage, especially when you know you are already booked and can't fit anything else into your schedule.

Busy vs. Effective Theory

One thing I feel strongly about is being effective by positively impacting other's lives. I've had to learn not to just be busy with no impact or results. Sometimes, you must stop and evaluate what you are doing. Ask yourself, "Am I just *being* busy, or am I *being* effective?" Look for the FRUIT! Look for the results of your actions.

Some things you are doing may not even be necessary. Or, maybe, you are so busy, you've double-booked yourself. Perhaps, you haven't learned how to say *no*, in a nice way to people, knowing that one more activity will "tip your plate over" (so to speak) and disrupt your healthy life balance.

So, take some time to re-evaluate your life and priorities. Be intentional about your purpose and your effectiveness!

3. Put YOU on your calendar

Make time for yourself! We tend to overlook one area of care, and that is "self-care." "Self-Care" is the hinge upon which all else in your life is balanced. If you don't take care of YOU, you will not be able to take care of anybody or anything else *you have on your plate*. Every month do something you enjoy. Put it on your calendar and don't cancel the appointment!

Remember: YOU are the most important thing on your calendar.

Reflection Page: *What things will you plan to do for yourself that will help you maintain your balance? Get your calendar out and start scheduling some time with yourself.*

DAY 21

~THE POWER OF CHOICE~

Choice – *the right, power, or opportunity to choose; options*

Every aspect of your life is based around or upon your choice. You choose where you will go to school, your career, where you will live, what type of car you will drive, what church you will attend, what you will wear or eat, who will be your friends, and who you will marry. These are just a few examples. Everything is a choice!

Every day when you wake up, you make a choice to either have a good day (Psalm 118:24), or murmur and complain, which sets the atmosphere to have a bad day. You have the power to choose to be happy, friendly, forgiving, encouraging, patient, supportive, loving, caring, and kind. Now, you can also choose to be the opposite of these traits—

unhappy, unfriendly, unforgiving, not encouraging, impatient, non-supportive, unloving, uncaring, and unkind. It is your choice, but you will have no one to blame but yourself if you choose to murmur and complain. You can choose to have *joy* and *peace* even when going through a difficult situation. You are the one who chooses how to react to situations and your attitude as you go through them.

"Choice" gives you the opportunity to be the thermostat, i.e., you establish and maintain the desired temperature and not the thermometer, i.e., seeking to find out the temperature. As the thermostat, you set the temperature. You decide it's going to be _____ today by commanding your morning and *speaking life* into your day. There is power in your words! *"The tongue has the power of life and death, and those who love it will eat its fruit."* Proverbs 18:21 (NIV). Make sure you speak LIFE, speak positive things. Choose to be happy! **You don't have to wait for something GOOD to happen to be happy. You have the power of choice! Choose wisely.**

Reflection Page: *Choose to be happy! Choose to succeed!*

DAY 22

~IT'S TIME TO EVICT FEAR AND DOUBT~

Fear is designed to paralyze you and keep you from "moving forward." Doubt causes you to question what God says.

Decide today that "fear" and "doubt" <u>will no longer hinder you</u> from being and doing all God has created you to be and do. It's time to "birth" those seeds of greatness that are inside of you.

Aren't you tired of being stagnant? Stagnation leads to "stinking thinking," which leads to you sabotaging yourself by speaking out negative words.

One day while I was at the gym, the Holy Spirit dropped this into my spirit:

FEAR = <u>F</u>ocused <u>E</u>nergy <u>A</u>round <u>R</u>eality

When you focus on your surroundings instead of the Word of God, fear will arise. Focus on God and stand on His Word. God cannot lie, and He is faithful! The promises of God are "Yes" and "Amen."

Fear wants you to quit, abort, and *throw in the towel*. Fear will say a lot of things, **but what does God say?** Don't be paralyzed by fear! Fear is designed to stop you from moving forward. Fear is the direct enemy of greatness. In order to do great things, you have to get rid of fear. *"For God hath not given us the spirit of fear; but of power, and of love, and of a sound mind."* 2 Timothy 1:7 (KJV).

Faith conquers fear! Combat the lies of fear with your faith and the Word of God. Feed your FAITH, and fear will disappear. Trust God, and then watch Him move on your behalf. Walk by faith today!

EVICT fear and doubt! Start speaking life! Don't walk by sight and begin living a fulfilled and purposeful life!

Reflection Page: *Make today the last day that fear and doubt will reside in you! What will you no longer allow fear to stop you from doing this week?*

DAY 23

~BE YOU~

Each of you is a unique individual. You were created with purpose. Your gifts, personality, and natural skill sets are designed to help you fulfill your purpose. You have to remember the "Potter" knows what He is creating and what function it will serve. As the clay, you need to trust that God has a plan for your life and submit to His will and design.

Don't compare yourself to others. Each of you has your own purpose, one that only you can get done. Nobody can accomplish your purpose but you! You were "wired" the way you are because of the purpose you have to fulfill. Stay in your lane and do what you were created and gifted to do!

Don't try to be somebody else. Be your "unique" self. You are an original masterpiece; never try to be a copy.

Make your own sound. Think about music for a second. If everyone played the same note or sang the same note, there would be no harmony. Just like an orchestra, each instrumental section has its own sound but when combined with all the other sections, it becomes a beautiful sounding orchestra. Play your note in life.

Don't apologize for who you are. Be you, unapologetically. You are fearfully and wonderfully made. God had intentional plans when He designed you. The only way you can truly be effective is to truly be yourself! **So, just be YOU!**

Reflection Page: *Don't "dis" God! God is the Potter, and we are the clay. Enjoy being your "unique" self!*

DAY 24

~FUEL YOUR MOTIVATION~

Just like a car needs fuel in order to run, so do your dreams. You must fuel your motivation, so you will continue to drive toward your dreams. Here are some tips to "fuel your motivation":

Have a visual goal

Keep your vision before you. A "Vision Board," a **board** on which you display pictures or images that represent whatever you want to be, do, or have in life, helps you stay focused on your goals and what you want to accomplish.

Speak life

It is important that as you create and write your vision, you are careful how and what you speak. You will either speak creatively (positive) or destructively (negative). What you speak is what you will draw toward you. Part of your creative power is the power of your words! Say, "I will _____ (finish school, start my business, write my book, etc.)."

Create – *To cause to exist; bring into being*

In creation, God spoke things into existence. He used His words. (See Genesis 1:1-26.) What words are you speaking? Speak words of affirmation that are related to your vision every morning.

Invest in your dreams

Learn more about what you want to do. Take courses, get a mentor, and attend seminars or workshops. Talk to people who are already doing what you want to do. **We invest in everything else; why not invest in your own dreams?**

Surround yourself with positive people

Keep positive people around you who will encourage you and support you as you work toward your goals and dreams. People who will not allow you to quit. It is very important to have "Dream Catchers" around you and not "Dream Drainers."

Plan how you will celebrate

How will you celebrate once your dream or dreams come to fruition? <u>Don't forget to celebrate your steps of accomplishment along the way</u>. It is like putting "premium gas" in your car's gas tank. Celebrating your steps along the way keeps you excited about your future!

> Now is the time to create that business, ministry, book, or whatever your "vision" is. It's time to say *deuces to excuses*. **Now, go and be unstoppable!**

Reflection Page: *Write down your vision. How will you invest in your goals and dreams? How will you celebrate each stage of your success?*

DAY 25

~BE UNSTOPPABLE!!~

Are you unstoppable, or do you "break" for every distraction that pops up?

Unstoppable - *Not capable of being stopped*

An unstoppable person has a plan and operates strategically to ensure his or her success. They are a master of "defusing distractions." Some characteristics of an "unstoppable" person are:

- Determined mind-Their mind is made up! - We know the mind is the strongest battlefield area. In other words, where our thoughts go, we go. If you don't make up your mind to be unstoppable, you won't be.
- Focused- This person looks forward not at their past and not at what everyone else is doing. They are not easily distracted.
- Strong support group- These people understand your vision and help you move forward. They encourage you, "speak life" to you, and pray for you.

Three things I've found helpful to stay focused:

Accountability

When you have accountability, you are more apt to get things done and will continue to work toward your goal or goals.

Deadlines

When you leave no target or end date for your goals, they just stay open or unfinished. There is no sense of urgency. But, when you set deadlines, you continually work toward that goal, so the deadline is met.

Guarding your time

Be aware of *Time Robbers*. Most people don't value your time. You have to either make them value your time or don't give them so much of your time. You have things to get done!

Reflection Page: *Start applying these tips on staying focused and see how productive you become. Which "tip" do you need to start with first?*

DAY 26

~CONFIDENCE BUILDER~

One thing I have learned is the importance of confidence. This was an area I struggled with, often combatting fear and doubt.

Five Confidence Builders that are very helpful:

1. Positive attitude
It's important to have a positive mindset. Negativity is the enemy of confidence. Negativity plants the seeds for doubt. You have to believe in yourself, and others will believe in you.

2. Eliminate excuses
Instead of making excuses, make moves. Instead of saying why you can't do something, talk about how you can and why you should do that very thing. Excuses can become "vision blockers." (Example…I'm too old to go back to school. I don't have the time to do that. I don't know how to start my own business. Where will I get the money? I don't have anyone to help me.) These "blockers" impede your progress. Confident people eliminate excuses which enables them to be successful.

3. Preparation
Being prepared is a great confidence booster. When you are prepared, it quiets fear. You are ready to face that meeting, interview, presentation, speaking engagement, etc. If you fail to plan and prepare, then you plan to fail.

4. Appearance
I know the inside is more important than the outside, but we still must maintain the outside. Grooming is important. Get your hair done, keep your nails clean and manicured, get your eyebrows arched, etc. Take care of yourself. When you look good, you feel good! Your confidence is high, and you perform on a high level. You represent your *brand* well. Always remember, when people see you, what will they think of your brand?

5. Dress to impress
There used to be a saying, "Dress for where you're going." Where are you going? Are you a professional? If you are, then dress like a professional. What you wear changes your mood. For example, when I have on a suit, I feel like taking care of business. When I have on sweat pants, I feel relaxed. How do you want your customer or client to see you? What do you want their first impression to be?

Here's an acronym for confidence:

C - Capable
O - Optimistic
N - Not negative
F-Focused
I -Invests in themselves
D-Determined /Does not doubt
E -Eliminates excuses
N - Never comparing
T - Teachable /Always willing to learn and grow

BE CONFIDENT - MOVE FORWARD!

Reflection Page: *Do you struggle with confidence? Which "Confidence Builder" will you apply this week?*

DAY 27

~TEMPERATURE CHECK~

When my children were growing up, I would periodically schedule time to meet with them to see how things were going in their life. I called this a "temperature check." We would discuss what challenges they were facing, what was going well, and what their plans were going forward.

As leaders, we do the same thing in corporate America. We conduct monthly one-on-one coaching discussions in order to see where we are with our goals. These sessions help us determine what we need to do to ensure we reach these goals by the end of the year.

As a Certified Life & Christian coach, I am checking in with you this month. What were the goals you wrote down earlier this year? Where are you in achieving these goals?
Are you HOT? - You are moving forward and getting things done.
Are you LUKEWARM? - You are sometimes moving forward, and then sometimes, you just stop.
Are you COLD? - You have stopped completely.

If you "fell off," it's okay; **you can regroup and**

restart. Get someone to be accountable to. Set realistic goals and timelines to help you stay on task. Identify what caused you to stop moving forward and create a plan, so you're not hindered again. Try to **avoid making excuses and make adjustments instead**.

Reflection Page: *What is your temperature?*

DAY 28

~DON'T GIVE UP~

Have you become weary? Have you asked when will it be my turn? Do you feel like you're doing all you're supposed to do, yet you still aren't getting ahead? If we're honest, we all feel like this at some point in our lives.

Galatians 6:9 (NIV) states, "*Let us not become weary in doing good, for at the proper time (or in due season) we will reap a harvest if we do not give up.*"
We all know we will become weary in doing good. But, I want to encourage you not to give up and FOCUS on the "due season!"

What does ***due*** mean? (www.merriam-webster.com) defines the word *due* as: *payable immediately or on demand; owed as a debt; in accord with right convention, or courtesy, appropriate.* It also means *meeting special requirements; sufficient;* **expected or scheduled; appointed to arrive; something that is owed or deserved.**

Continue doing good, what God has told you to do, and you WILL REAP in your "due season." You can expect to reap. It is owed you and appointed to arrive in God's timing-on demand! You are meeting the "special requirements" by continuing to do good.
The key is **not to give up**.

What can you do to keep from giving up?

- Trust God & believe His promises

    2 Corinthians 1:20 (NIV) *"For no matter how many promises God has made, they are 'Yes' in Christ. And so through him the 'Amen' is spoken by us to the glory of God."*

    Hebrews 10:23 (NIV) *"Let us hold unswervingly to the hope we profess, for he who promised is faithful."*

- Encourage and sharpen one another

    Hebrews 3:13 (NIV) *"But encourage one another daily, as long as it is called 'Today,' so that none of you may be hardened by sin's deceitfulness."*

    Hebrews 10:25 (NIV) *"not giving up meeting together, as some are in the habit of doing, but encouraging one another – and all the more as you see the Day approaching."*

- Expect Your **"due season"**

    1 Corinthians 2:9 (NIV) *"However, as it is written: 'What no eye has seen, what no ear has heard, and what no human mind has conceived'– the things God has prepared for those who love him--"*

Remember, Satan wants us to get weary and quit and forfeit what is owed or due us. **Continue to be faithful, keep doing "good," and expect your "due season."**

Reflection Page: *Don't Give Up! The reality is we all get weary, but we can't quit!*

DAY 29

~LAST LAP~

My oldest son used to run cross country when he was in high school. One detail I noticed is the runners would pace themselves when they first started the race, keeping a nice, steady pace as they ran their laps. They would reserve some energy for the "last lap" and home stretch. You may be in the last phase of bringing your vision to fruition. Hopefully, you have reserved some energy for the home stretch. Remember, the race is not given to the swift but to those who endure to the end.

What things do you need to get done? You can get them done as you stretch your legs and put everything into the last lap. You will come down the home stretch and successfully complete turning your dreams into reality. Don't allow the enemy to derail you when you are so close to the finish line! According to Philippians 4:13, ***you can do ALL things through Jesus Christ who gives you strength!***

Ding-Ding That's the bell indicating the last lap to complete your vision or dreams has begun. I will see you, victoriously, at the finish line!

Reflection Page: *What are some things you need to get done? How will you pace yourself, so you can reserve energy for the final stages of completing your goal?*

DAY 30

~IT'S TIME FOR SOME ACTION!~

You have been planning and preparing. Now, it's time to manifest.

It's time to put some feet to your plans. Writing the vision is one thing but walking out the vision is another. If you have properly planned and will step out in faith, with God's leading, your vision will begin to manifest. God always provides provision for the vision.

It' time to be a "water-walker!" You have to come out of the boat (your comfort zone) and take a step of faith. Peter would have never walked on water if he allowed fear to stop him. Fear is the biggest blocker to greatness. Peter did not worry about what the other eleven disciples did; he obeyed God's voice when He told him, "Come." (See Matthew 14:29.)

You, too, will have to hear God's voice above any other voices and not be concerned about what everyone else does or doesn't do. **Step out of the boat and into your destiny!**

Reflection Page: *What will you step out and do this week?*

DAY 31

~A DRIVING FORCE BEHIND SUCCESS~

Every time I listen to an interview about successful people, almost all of them have one common denominator - **Perseverance.**

Persevere- *to persist in or remain constant to a purpose, idea, or task* **in the face of obstacles or discouragement.**

We see people celebrating their success, but <u>we don't know the struggles they faced during the process</u>. You see my "glory," but you don't know my "story." We don't know how many times they tried and were rejected **but <u>refused</u> to give up!** They persevered and continued, trying until somebody said," Yes." **Quitting was not an option for them.** They believed in their dreams & visions and had a tenacious mindset to see them come to fruition. They faced many obstacles and challenges, but they did not allow that to STOP them from moving forward.

After listening to these interviews, I realized <u>without perseverance, you're guaranteed to quit</u>. There will be obstacles or challenges but don't allow anything to impede your progress and eventually kill your dreams.

What are your dreams or vision? Are you willing to persevere to see them come to fruition?

I encourage you to continue **moving forward**. Continue to pursue your dreams. Focus your time and energy on things that line up with your vision. Don't allow "vision blockers" to stop you! Regain VISION and CLARITY and MOVE FORWARD! Remember, the only person with the power to stop you - is YOU.

Reflection Page: *Are you <u>committed</u> to seeing your dreams come to fruition?*

"ARE YOU COMMITTED?"

Have you noticed that people just aren't committed to anything lately?
Whether it's our relationships, i.e., God, family, or friendships, our jobs, our church, or our projects, we have a hard time staying committed and following through. This is a big character flaw. People don't support each other even if they say they will. They do what they want to do regardless of what they say they will do. Even if they have committed or promised to do something, nowadays, a person's word is no longer their bond.

Why is this an issue?

First of all, it blemishes your character, your integrity, and your name. The Bible says we are to let our, "Yes" be "Yes" and our, "No" be "No" according to Matthew 5:37. When you commit or tell someone, YES about something, you should carry out that YES unless you are providentially hindered. Your plans shouldn't change simply because something came up you would rather do. **This is a character issue, making your word worthless!**

In years past, a contract or agreement was made based on a person's word and their hand shake. Children were known because of their family name. The parents' character paved a way for their children. **We cannot do that today! Shame on us, as <u>Christians,</u> if people can't trust or depend on our word.** Proverbs 22:1 (NIV) says, "*A good name is more desirable than great riches;*"

Uncommitted behavior gives you a bad name. Your words can't be trusted and definitely <u>not</u> depended upon. People have become so used to saying or promising one thing and doing another, they don't even realize they are doing it.

People should be able to say, "If _____ (put your name here) said it, then he or she will be here or do it (what they promised)." People should know *your word is good!* People should not have to wonder if you will follow through.

Secondly, and most importantly, this behavior is contradictory to **the Word of God!**
Being uncommitted is not Christ-like and does not set a good example for unbelievers (those in the world). We are supposed to be "light," an example and an advertisement for Jesus Christ.

What are people seeing through you and your actions? What perception of Jesus Christ are people seeing from your example?

Choose today to change this unholy behavior. Let

your *yes* be *yes* and your *no* be *no*. Have a "good name," <u>one people can trust and depend on</u>. Be committed to the people and things you have said, "Yes" to. **Having a *good name* and character is important for you and your children.**

Reflection Page: *What areas in your life have you been uncommitted?*

THE POWER OF ENCOURAGEMENT

Encouragement has the power to push a person past their pain, give them the energy to keep going, and the determination not to quit. Encouragement has the power to fuel and motivate success! I hope my book has done this for you!

Encourage your family, friends, co-workers, teacher, neighbor, and church members to get this book, so they can be motivated to move forward.

Speak a word of encouragement to someone today. You don't know what a difference it will make in their life.

Reflection Page: *Write down how you felt giving words of encouragement to someone. How did it make the other person feel?*

A SPECIAL THANKS

I would like to thank my husband Henry L. Brailey, Jr. for all his love and support. He has always believed in me and has never allowed me to quit on my dreams. I would also like to thank him for keeping me balanced and ensuring that I had times to relax when I started to feel overwhelmed.

I would like to thank my mother, Sandra Faye Davis for being my spiritual mid-wife telling me when to breathe and when to push, keeping me focused and organized, praying for me daily, and sending me words of encouragement which always seemed to be right on time.

I would like to thank my children Tynesha Chandler-Allsop, Terence Lamar Chandler, and Terrell Chandler for always believing in me and making me feel like I can do anything. Encouraging me to make my dreams become a reality!

I also want to thank Linda McMichael and Donna Peace for being " Dream Catchers," allowing me to share my dreams and vision with them , for holding me accountable, encouraging me on days when I was on "E," and for fueling my motivation.

This is my inner circle.

I want to thank each one of you for all your prayers and support!

I love you!

ABOUT THE AUTHOR

As a <u>Life</u> Coach Shyron desires to help "**Move YOU Forward**" so you can achieve your goal/s. Getting you out of that stuck or holding pattern in your life and into motion towards achieving your goal/s. Shyron partners with you on your journey to success. Assisting you in identifying your vision blockers. Helping you to come up with a strategy to remove those blockers and regain vision clarity as well as motivation to Move Forward. You can count on Shyron to provide you with accountability and encouragement throughout your journey to success.

As a <u>HIS Coach</u> *(Spirit-led Christian Coach)* Shyron desires to see you grow in the Lord.
First by discovering the root cause/s of your actions and dealing with them according to the Word of God. So you can truly be FREE to "Move Forward" in your relationship with God and in your divine purpose.

Secondly, through transformational teaching which includes 3 simple steps "LEARN-APPLY-GROW". Shyron teaches in a way that is easy to understand and to apply to your life. Teachings to help you grow and mature in your Christian walk.

As a Life & Christian Coach my ultimate goal for you is RESULTS!

Mrs. Shyron G. Brailey
Certified Life & Christian Coach | CCRMC | Speaker

Coaching For Success, LLC
Email: shyronbrailey@coachinguforsuccess.com
Website: www.coachinguforsuccess.com
Facebook: www.facebook.com/coachinguforsuccess
P.O. Box 836 Knightdale, NC 27545

ABOUT ZION PUBLISHING HOUSE

ZION Publishing House is a family-owned publishing company based in Southern California and Washington, DC. ZION helps Christian authors tell their stories by providing an affordable alternative to traditional publishing. Our mission is to maintain a platform that educates and empowers independent Christian authors. We do this by cultivating talent in the inspirational and self-help genres for novice and experienced authors. The path to publishing can be daunting and extremely complex. We take pride in taking our clients by the hand and walking them through the publishing process to ensure they not only have a high-quality product that resonates with the reader, but they understand the many facets of the publishing industry and what it means to be a published author.

If you are a writer looking for an affordable path to publishing, visit our website at www.zionpublishinghouse.com to learn more.

www.ingramcontent.com/pod-product-compliance
Lightning Source LLC
Chambersburg PA
CBHW020426010526
44118CB00010B/446